www.finishinglinepress.com

This Is the Syntax Called Bettie Page

poems by

Melissa Morphew

Finishing Line Press
Georgetown, Kentucky

This Is the Syntax Called Bettie Page

ACKNOWLEDGMENTS

Some of these poems were printed previously in the following journals/
anthologies—sometimes in earlier versions.

Her Texas: Story, Image, Poem, and Song: "Dallas, 1959;" "A Short History
of the Cold War;" and "As if Our Lives Starred Joanne Woodward & Paul
Newman in a Script by Carson McCullers"
Pea River Journal: "The Role of a Lifetime, 1964;" "You Left, And;" "This
Is the Syntax Called Bettie Page;" and "Left, Then Right, She Followed the
Twisting Turns of Mulholland—Nothing Seemed Extraordinary Until the
Moment of Impact"
Poet Lore: "Diane Arbus's Ghost Tells It Straight"

Publisher: Leah Maines
Editor: Christen Kincaid
Cover Art: https://unsplash.com/license; Greg Kantra
Author Photo: Melissa Morphew
Cover Design: Elizabeth Maines McCleavy

Printed in the USA on acid-free paper.
Order online: www.finishinglinepress.com
also available on amazon.com

Author inquiries and mail orders:
Finishing Line Press
P. O. Box 1626
Georgetown, Kentucky 40324
U. S. A.

Table of Contents

*This book is dedicated to Sandra Dee and Hayley Mills
and all the girls who loved them*

This Is the Syntax Called Bettie Page

Even as a child, I learned
the importance of beauty, every

spring, fall—that knowledge
a privilege. I remember

when I was seven, my father
told me "you radiate penstemon light—a wild

pink snapdragon perpetually posed
as bee-swelled kiss." Those words

like pollen-dust, a stamen-sweet prize. Ecstatic—
a lace collar lit my face, my black hair

softly clasped in gold barrettes. *The perfect
little girl*—innocent, irresistible,

unapproachable. The looks. The whispers.
I pretended those stairs led to a bedroom

of white-curtained windows.
                              I was shy,

wanted to dance, graceful
ballerina, *straight and sleek*, to starve myself.

That summer I turned 14, stalled
on the corner before I went in, chewing four

Dubble Bubbles, the start of a roller-coaster year.
An angel napped under the umbrella-sunset, checking out

the topless women of Boca Raton; misspelled sister-notes:
He's so cute I can barely stand—it makes me hunger.

Everyone kept me in dark, red-lit rooms
from beginning to end. I spent half the time thinking—

It's my birthday! Blow out the candles. Nothing has
changed—rose-dolloped cake, dime-store presents, silver confetti,

fever. I want to know what that future
                                        may not hold.

The Melodramatic Scene in Which We Resist What We Can Change in Favor of the Impossible

We equal what we never say—in a grown-up game
of rock, paper, scissors. Is love what we are?
White flowers on an altar, frosted organdy,
mousseline de soie?

Do you remember that winter? We spoke of pearls,
candlesticks and ashtrays, anniversaries—
how the second year is cotton, the sixth year—iron,
by the eleventh—steel. Bride of pillowcases, salt cellars,
garden shears and knives.

In the oyster farms of Japan, female divers plunge
to death-defying depths for baubles they'll never wear. Every day
at the Y, I think of them, sink
to the bottom of the pool, hold my breath
longer and longer.

Douglas Sirk could film us, 24 frames a second,
144,000 frames to sum up this quiet desperation,
broken vows and inconstancy. Hollywood offers
these transitory dreams, a perfection half-full,
a truth half-empty, and we are mesmerized by soap flakes
in the guise of snow.

Take 12: Mother Finds Receipt for Pierre Hotel in Pocket of Father's Navy Serge Suit

It's odd how history is an occasional
cloud that hovers over our dinner table,

and suddenly mother's white dress afire in the doorway,
her tone-deaf hands puzzling out

months of paper insights as time
follows a trail of bread crumbs, juniper berries,

broken rubber bands. Monks in India
noticed specific words show up

again and again in Pali, Sanskrit, Chinese—
antecedent of long lost siblings not yet found.

April afternoons and the corner mailbox empty—
a dark cavern easily filled with yellow tulips,

caramel nougat bonbons in a pink foil box—
a number as far back as the record goes

sugar-violet blue, forgotten
in the first place. A persistent quarrel

tells us something interesting, important.
I heard who this was. She had three-inch

lacquered heels, a bracelet with bells, a green silk
dress cut just above the knee—the account,

the story others had missed, wants to claim
its foothold, Gnostic gospel

that will never fit in her mouth,
the wall she can't put her fist through,

report of weather, holding.

Asunder

She listens for the story, the private
narrative of her body burned

by a blaze of nasturtiums,
her garden's curved geometry,

pale-purple violets seeded thick as stars,
clandestine language of unthinkable sorrow

edged in a May wind, a prayer of uncertain bloom,
to ask this green-bright question—was she

simply the echo of his ribs? the jailed honeycomb?
And how can she endure this soap-strict reckoning, physics

of separation, the one hundred phone calls
she will not make to tell him

the Japanese iris exposed its roots,
the record player broke its stylus; each evening

this cloud-smeared music keeps time in silence,
counts backward.

Diane Arbus's Ghost Tells It Straight

I would have made a fine photograph—

woman mermaided in the bloody water of the tub,
just a hint of the outline of my breasts,

the black and white tiles suggestive
of a chessboard, the game of course—

death. And no need to ask,
I would have lit the room to imply

the afternoon's dull blues, the July heat,
found the proper aperture to emphasize

the cold cream jars, shampoo bottles,
tooth-paste-spattered bric-a-brac,

and somehow softened this slit-wrist suicide—
a trick of still-life domesticity

to cloud the lens—my razored-wit
off-center, but not abnormal—

this final image—a pixie-shorn female,
eyes wide, staring off—perhaps daydreaming,

perhaps planning a simple supper
of scrambled eggs and toast.

If only there'd been curlers in my hair,
a cigarette smoldering in an ashtray,

a hunchbacked twin perched on the toilet
chit-chatting, filing her nails.

When She Plays This Scene as if Billy Wilder Directs the Ingénue Shirley MacLaine

Blood on the sheets tells a story. Why don't you figure it out?

In her room at the Pink Dolphin hotel, she acts
the part of sweet charity—all cheekbones & doe eyes,

a bell-curve show & tell, poised elegance
in movie-siren shades.

Her suitcase a language
of worn velvet gloves, a lace cloth-bag covered in satin roses,

the little black dress, thigh-high black boots
& fishnet tights—

Do I travel light? Never—
I mean, I'm not sad.

Tepid white tulips in a bathroom glass
perched on her nightstand—yearning allure of monsoon,

winter afternoons, lunar seas, that cigarette-after-cigarette
season of secrets left ajar,

houseboys
scurrying in silver syllables through the tangerine heat.

An unexpected necklace of *millifiori* purchased
at an airport kiosk, a fire-escape sort of gift,

the shattered-voices-against-the-windows-glamour
of a city moving to its own panic.

Old lovers
spike their goodbyes with gin, *Riviera joie de vivre,*

halter-topped girls
                    blonde as summer.

Back home in Kentucky, she could lunch on pickled eggs,
an RC Cola,

                    follow the railroad tracks
to the flooded dark of the Dunbar Mine—

                                        here
she's stuck—a needle in the torched-groove-resignation
of Edith Piaf, Nina Simone.

                    Really, I'm fine, just fine,
rolling moss & stones, etc., etc.—you know.

It's easy enough to get train fare when you have
somewhere to go. Something to sell along the way.

A Short History of the Cold War

I wanted to tell you the art
of eating chocolate was lost
in the "heady" days of Marie Antoinette
when Spanish oranges were spiced with cloves
and women tucked lavender sachets
between the talcum-dusted moons
of their breasts,
                but as usual
you cut me off with that not-again-
twitch of your left brow,
and now we sit here, each alone
in the granite-topped-coolness of our
February kitchen, glancing out windows
at the jittery birds. *What's that?*
                Yes, I suppose you're right, even my anger
tends toward the poetic, the calculated
metaphor that lets me assume meaning
still exits somewhere in our haphazard bric-a-brac.
                Do you think we might start over? Agree
to read the same books, listen
to the same bleak piano plink out
a Satie soundtrack to our silent walks,
make love at 4:00 o'clock
every Wednesday afternoon.
                Very funny, and how do you know
I won't forget to pencil *you* in,
to mark off the edges of a calendar
which seems more and more a parallel universe.
                I thought you wanted a poem, a painting
colored out in words, an endless conversation
that swirled into nebulas
and never grew old, but then like everyone
we ever knew, those fathers and mothers
with their happy hour martinis, garnished
with pearl onions and the chill of endless bickering,

we've settled into a routine,
moving through rooms as if in pantomime,
a couple in a silent movie, indelible
in grainy hues of black and white.

  Oh, so that's your answer—just leave, just pretend
the last fifteen years are someone else's story,
a documentary which could only play
in an art house theatre downtown because the plot
is nonexistent, it's just life, just life.

  And what am I supposed to do *now*? Forget
I love you, or is that too cliché, after all
we live in a postmodern world, and love
isn't the point. Where do you propose we go?
How do we end this? And where should I place
those years that still pulse through my dreams—
the summers at the beach, the way the sun
lit the room with blues, bleached whites,
and you kissed me and your kisses tasted
of wine, apples, the decadence of honeyed-brie.

  Tell me, how do I forget this life, comfortable
even in its bitterness?

  Tell me, how do I close this house for winter?

Dusk in the Garden Called Marilyn Monroe

Not for the honeybee

      to ever again
cross the anther of desire—to find you

with quickened eyes? a dialect of golden dust? to follow
a trail of loquat—Sri Lankan evergreens, fat with yellow plums?

And if I say—
      no, never mind, nothing . . .

I loved you once, long ago.

      But now it's winter—
sap sweetens the deepest cells of trees—
a stilled heartbeat, precarious, waiting
for the taut green of April.

      But where has April gone?

      The hive is dark.

      No longer will I come to you—
brimmed with sugar, stung.

The Role of a Lifetime—1964

The lost buttons of a hundred cities

crammed into drawerfuls of disorder,
conclusive proof of her wool skirts'

sequential carelessness, her cardigans'
beautiful descent into chaos theory
and décolletage.
                    Today
she's Yvette Mimieux, kittened-ingénue
of the blonde bombshells, penciled-tight

in pink cashmere, pearl-demured,
and loosely bobby-pinned, snug

in the fine weather of a Catalina-coastal landscape,
early May, the café table inscribed

with primrose and hawthorn, the green stutter
of bottle-flies, brushing against her teacup's

porcelain geometry.
                        And perhaps she's waiting
for some bank-job fugitive, a Parisian bad-boy,

all oiled-hair and unfiltered cigarettes, his repartee
staccato-gunfire aimed at shooting down

her white-flowered resolve to pedal back,
recast the last ten years and find the girl

she'd been, butterfly trapped in a jar
just this side of honey-bruised love, but *that* film

stars Jean Seberg;
                no, *she's* caught in a scurry
of perfume and kid-gloves, stray Kleenex

shredded at the bottom of her purse, salting away
the intrigue of clubhouse afternoons, circumstantial lovers,

luggage tucked into the front seat of her Oldsmobile
only to be lost in talk of Thursday apartments, a stunning
language of broken mirrors and slammed doors.

Her wristwatch remarks each second
with airy efficiency; stood up once again.

She thinks how somewhere at the edge
of the world the rainy season's begun,
weeks of monsoon,
                        jade-bright deluge,
tangerine fresh, baptismal.

You Left, And

           the sun stopped shining
on all the lakes of the world,

gray clouds descending
like fog, the grass dried,

yellowed, so every photograph
turned sepia, instant nostalgia

for a present we possessed as past
but couldn't walk backwards through

toward some meaning, some reticent understanding,
trace the last pink flower pressed

between pages of the family Bible,
this fragile reckoning written

in the parlance of love, this onionskin
memory, the words blurred,

smudged by too often turning
to the same page, never moving beyond

the stained crease of obsessive familiarity,
footsteps faint upon mahogany stairs,

the thermostat broken, the house empty
except for woolen blankets, heavy quilts,

wrought-iron beds, lumpy mattresses damp
with mildew—a talisman of loneliness—

not a single window, a single door
opening onto a garden,

some orchard made of light.

As if Our Lives Starred Joanne Woodward & Paul Newman in a Script by Carson McCullers

Nacogdoches June, the heat a steady pulse
like static on the radio, an AM station
siphoning Tejano music hundreds of miles from Mexico,
a spare love of spent heels and Lucky Strikes,
pinball machines and night-blooming jasmine,
a pink cotton dress forgotten on the clothesline,
sawdust settling on our skin.

We found Grandpa's Victrola in the attic,
filled the kitchen with the simmering crackle of Bob Wills
and the Texas Playboys at 78 rpms—records
with the heft of dinner plates.

What happened?

He bought me a Hershey bar, a cherry coke;
we snuck into the movies to see *Splendor in the Grass*.

You wouldn't understand.

A boy moved piles of dirt at the public
playground. He was seven or eight, wearing
a red and white striped t-shirt. One of his eyes
always seemed to be looking away, cocked
toward the western horizon.

You live in lala land girl. Got it—lala land.

What if I told you, we made love underneath
a rundown house—surrounded by JuicyFruit wrappers,
the skeletons of mice and baby birds—
his hands like sandpaper, and I
                                        was something hewn.

What if I told you, I ripped
out the carpets, painted
the walls blue, thankful
                    it only took one summer.

Left, Then Right, She Followed the Twisting Turns of Mulholland—
Nothing Seemed Extraordinary Until the Moment of Impact

           The party crowded, the women California-chic
in blood-orange silks and calabash-green satins,
a communion of gold-stubbed cigarettes festooning
the carved-coral ashtrays, the party-goers buried
a scant two years, smiling up from the vicious
distance of unmade afternoons, summer gossip,
fevered—black De Sotos tonguing the curb
of by-the-hour Malibu motels.
                June—cashmere-sweatered blonde, Bud's wife,
his thorn-in-the-side angel, his white-bone-of-moonlight-and-
ragged-fingernails, radiant
with the hushed-museum-sadness of a Flemish
masterpiece, dropped from another suspect planet,
the beggared alleyways of Ghent, swan-necked
and bitter—
           this novice to ruin, to the suffocation
of beehives and catacombs, this woman,
she, herself, would not recognize, so eager
to mention accomplishments, brief successes, Phi Beta Kappa,
a year in Provence, a romance thirty-years
from the East Coast, a sleek Spanish villa
snug in the heart of the Hollywood Hills—
                   June turned, lost.
     Can you believe, she said, her voice
an embarrassment of Rodgers and Hart resolve,
her left hand a game-show gesture of graceful spotlight,
that's a rendering of me.
             And if anyone had paused mid-word, mid-syllable,
looked up—they would have seen nothing, a white dress
burned against a charcoal mass of trees, a smile,
spare with cityscapes, verging on despair
to occupy a place wonderful as newspaper,
                      barely noticed books.
     She hadn't realized to marry was to enter

the candid pose of photographs, polaroid memorabilia,
to make scrapbooks of a star-tinged desert, lush
with ache and saguaros.

                    She dropped her hand—
this ghost at the cocktail party—suspended
in the smoke-burnished lilt of piano-jazz and small talk,
innuendo's mumbly laughter, haunting
the fringes of her own house, circling the backyard,
the patio, imploring her guests—What can I do?
Is there anything I can do?

Because I Knew He'd Love Me as Long as He Wanted

                    I got stuck—
living in a Podunk cow-town, one streetlight
and miles of dust—a place articulate as John Wayne
disarmed and drunk.

And I know about drunks—
how black-eyes become casual
as perfunctory kisses, dreadful
as perfunctory sex.

So I grabbed my keys,
mashed the accelerator, left behind all
the just-another-Mondays—part opium,
part woebegone distances—the backlit winter
of my dissembled life—the polite
how-are-yous? from friends and neighbors
that forced me to be *fine, just fine.*

White-knuckling the steering wheel,
I sped across sun-faded flatlands aiming
for the western horizon. Not a stick of luggage,
just a pair of kick-ass, stiletto-heeled boots,
a pack of Woodbines, Patsy Cline's vaulting octaves
dissolving in and out of the radio.

           I inherited a piano from my Grandma Dixie; her showbiz name
was Denise. She gave me the piano to remember
sometimes leaving's the only choice. I guess she knew
where I was headed. Las Vegas loomed in my windshield,

                              the skyline
inching closer and closer. I swerved into the airport parking lot,
running on fumes. Christmas Eve 1966. Flat broke, not even
a sticky, lint-covered quarter to play the slots, but in possession

of the only thing that mattered—a dog-eared, one-way ticket
that would whisk me away to nowhere in particular
as long as it was somewhere else.

In the passenger lounge, carolers drifted to and fro,
singing Bing Crosby standards or Nat King Cole,
festive tunes that made me uncomfortable. I preferred
the heartbreak croon of "Crazy" or "I Fall to Pieces"—and I did—
fall to pieces—sank into the half-light of the bar—the boozy-fumes
of spilled whiskey—and sobbed—ugly-snotty-tears
that knocked the air right out of my chest.

A waitress handed me a Santa napkin. *There, there, honey.*
Just catch your breath. Christmas? It's a bitch, right?
Brings all the awful to the surface. But you'll survive,
I promise. I've been there—I know. Ladies room is that way
if you want to fix your mascara, powder your nose.

Dallas, 1959

Our house, this museum of summer's
voluptuous heliotrope—boundaries
of flowerboxes delinquent with spent amaryllis—

we lounge beside the pool, nameless
travelers tempted to exchanges of soliloquy,
the indolent blah-blah of weathered postcards.

I want to tell you how, once, the sky unfolded
mantis-green, dissolving into a reverberation of storm,
and I let the screen door slam behind me,

rushed outside, the silver maples an incomprehensible
panic of limbs and leaves invented
between camera-flashes of lightning.

The same way you invented me with the economy
of your kisses, those resinous hours
trapped inside the persistent architecture

of glass-front buildings, chrome-gilded Cadillacs,
tea parties backdropped by purple orchids
and talk of money. Our marriage

a science of country air and oceanfront property,
traces of birdsong settling the trees, the simplest
moments clothed in autumn lanes, perspicacious bishops.

Compotes and comfits—the currency of pleasantries. And my
recurring dream, a woman in a blue skirt making her way
through an endless field of cornflower, arms spread wide.

Melissa Morphew is a native Southerner and a graduate of the University of Georgia's PhD program. True to her roots, she has crisscrossed the south, teaching creative writing and English literature, in various states, including Tennessee, Georgia, South Carolina, Texas, and Alabama. She has published five previous poetry collections: *Hunger and Heat (The Missionary Letters), The Garden Where All Loves End, Fathom, Weeding Borges' Garden,* and *Bluster.* Over the years, her poems have appeared in many national and international poetry journals such as *The Georgia Review, Shenandoah, Prairie Schooner, Crab Orchard Review, Poet Lore, Seneca Review, The Alaska Quarterly,* etc. She is the recipient of a Sacramento Poetry Center Press Book Award, a W.B. Yeats Society Poetry Prize, a Randall Jarrell International Poetry Prize, and a Tennessee Arts Commission Grant in Poetry, among other awards and honors. She currently teaches in the Professional Studies Program at the University of Alabama in Huntsville.

www.ingramcontent.com/pod-product-compliance
Lightning Source LLC
LaVergne TN
LVHW021128080426
835510LV00021B/3355